LEAPS
In Times of Anger

Edited by
Phil Etienne

Illustrated by
Randy Wollenmann

ONE
CARING
PLACE

Abbey Press
St. Meinrad, IN 47577

Text © 2003 Abbey Press
Illustrations © 2003 St. Meinrad Archabbey
Published by One Caring Place
Abbey Press
St. Meinrad, Indiana 47577

Library of Congress Catalog Number
2003101265

ISBN 0-87029-373-7

Printed in the United States of America

Foreword

If ever there was a list of emotions that conjure up the worst in us, anger would be at the top of it. From a child in full-blown temper tantrum mode, to an adult's equivalent in the midst of a heated argument, to the seemingly trivial everyday challenges, the images associated with anger are, without a doubt, our least flattering. And beyond the embarrassing contortions, uncontrollable anger can be truly harmful to us and those around us.

Therefore, we often strive to control—even eliminate—anger from our lives. But, anger is an unavoidable part of humanity. When we attempt to suppress anger or ignore it, we are equally harmful to our physical and mental well-being…and, to others'.

So, how can we release our anger in a constructive way, without all the accompanying messiness? While there's no sure-fire recipe for success, we can draw upon others' knowledge on this subject and draw upon our faith. From our many publications addressing this topic, we have mined nuggets of wisdom for dealing with anger. Accompanied with Scripture quotes, and highlighted with illustrations, these brief, thought-provoking insights help readers embrace the positive aspects of anger and find a comfortable co-existence with our sometimes surly selves!

A certain amount of anger is good—
often necessary for our survival.

"My heart is indeed like wine that
has no vent; like new wineskins, it is
ready to burst. I must speak,
so that I may find relief; I
must open my lips and answer."
—Job 32:19-20

Anger is a natural, God-given experience that can serve us well when we relate with it in constructive ways.

"For His anger is but for a moment, His favor is for a lifetime; Weeping may last for the night, But a shout of joy {comes} in the morning."

—Psalms 30:5

Acknowledge to yourself and others in the situation that you are angry. Be willing to actually say, "I am really mad!"

"Therefore I will not restrain my mouth; I will speak in the anguish of my spirit; I will complain in the bitterness of my soul."

—Job 7:11

When we're embarrassed or ashamed of our anger, we only bring more issues into the chaos. By stating that we're angry, we respect our own inner experience while communicating to others the reality of the situation.

"I loathe my life; I will give free utterance to my complaint; I will speak in the bitterness of my soul."
—Job 10:1

When we allow our anger to control our behavior, we are at risk of wreaking psychological or physical damage on ourselves and others.

"I the Lord test the mind
and search the heart, to
give to all according to
their ways, according to
the fruit of their doings."
—Jeremiah 17:10

Some of our angriest moments are when "the same old thing" has happened again: the toilet seat is left up—again; another driver "cuts us off" or takes up two parking spaces—again.

"Refrain from anger, and forsake wrath. Do not fret—it leads only to evil."

—Psalms 37:8

The circumstances that generate anger usually give rise to other emotions that precede anger; anger simply has a much higher and more conscious energy to it.

"He who is slow to anger is better than the mighty, And he who rules his spirit, than he who captures a city."

—Proverbs 16:32

When we acknowledge that we're angry, state why we're angry, and know the emotions that precede our anger, we are able to consider all the facts in the situation.

"Who is like the wise man? And who knows the interpretation of a thing? Wisdom makes one's face shine, and the hardness of one's countenance is changed."
—Ecclesiastes 8:1

Anger can help you speak your truth assertively and get your needs met.

"The Lord is near to all who call on him, to all who call on him in truth."

—Psalms 145:18

Too often, we think of anger as a tool that we can use to manipulate a situation. But anger does not change facts, and facts are what have generated our anger.

"A hot-tempered man stirs up strife, But the slow to anger calms a dispute."

—Proverbs 15:18

Many people confuse anger with aggression. But anger is not aggression. Anger is something we feel; aggression is something we do. As an emotion, anger can be expressed in many ways, constructively or destructively.

"Let my accusers be put to shame and consumed; let those who seek to hurt me be covered with scorn and disgrace."

—Psalms 71:13

Some people don't admit to anger in the first place. They act like martyrs, breeding guilt in those around them.

"Lament and mourn and weep. Let your laughter be turned into mourning and your joy into dejection."

—James 4:9

Express your anger assertively. Assertive anger is the one method that communicates our needs and feelings without violating the integrity of others.

"Let no evil talk come out of your mouths, but only what is useful for building up, as there is need, so that your words may give grace to those who hear."

—Ephesians 4:29

When we express anger assertively, we state clearly and firmly what is upsetting us, without attacking the other person.

"Show yourself in all respects a model of good works, and in your teaching show integrity, gravity, and sound speech that cannot be censured; then any opponent will be put to shame, having nothing evil to say of us."
—Titus 2:7-8

Clarify the real issue. Stop, take a deep breath, and ask yourself, "What am I thinking and feeling?" "What about this situation makes me angry?" "What am I really angry about?"

"But truly it is the spirit in a mortal, the breath of the Almighty, that makes for understanding. It is not the old that are wise, nor the aged that understand what is right. Therefore I say, 'Listen to me; let me also declare my opinion.'"

—Job 32:8-10

Slow down! In the midst of anger, we often speak impulsively. Slowing down allows us to disengage and stay calm.

"A man's discretion makes him slow to anger, And it is his glory to overlook a transgression."

—Proverbs 19:11

It's important to distinguish between recognizing anger and venting it. Simply venting anger for its own sake rarely brings about lasting change.

"{This} you know, my beloved brethren. But everyone must be quick to hear, slow to speak {and} slow to anger; for the anger of man does not achieve the righteousness of God."

—James 1:19-20

In conflict situations, people tend to shut down. Unfortunately, this only escalates the anger. Stay open and continue to engage.

"A gentle answer turns away wrath, But a harsh word stirs up anger."

—Proverbs 15:1

Let go of anger in situations you can't control. Trying to change another person or circumstances over which you have no control leaves you frustrated and with reduced energy to exercise the power you do have.

"Let all bitterness and wrath and anger and clamor and slander be put away from you, along with all malice."
—Ephesians 4:31

Holding in your anger requires a lot of energy. Sharing your anger, in words or in writing—with another person, with God—frees up that energy for more constructive uses.

"Be angry, and {yet} do not sin; do not let the sun go down on your anger..."

—Ephesians 4:26

Exercise—whether walking, running, biking, or swimming—helps the body release its pent-up desire to lash out in anger. The workout will help your heart in more ways than one.

"O you who tear yourself in your anger—For your sake is the earth to be abandoned, Or the rock to be moved from its place?"

—Job 18:4

Anger at its best is a dialogue. Through anger, you can touch another and you can be touched, bridging the solitudes of two unique persons with healing love.

"So then, putting away falsehood, let all of us speak the truth to our neighbors, for we are members of one another."

—Ephesians 4:25

Forgiveness and anger can reside together within the human heart. God's grace, available to all of us, transforms human anger so that there is room for forgiveness.

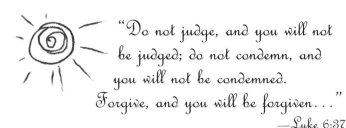

"Do not judge, and you will not be judged; do not condemn, and you will not be condemned. Forgive, and you will be forgiven..."
—Luke 6:37

Next time strong feelings of anger arise, stop for a minute and realize you have a choice in how you will proceed.

"He who is slow to anger has great understanding, But he who is quick-tempered exalts folly."
—Proverbs 14:29

If you really blow up, apologize, try to clear up any damage you've done, and resolve to do better next time. Back up that resolve with behavior changes that lessen the likelihood of a recurrence.

"But now you also, put them all aside: anger, wrath, malice, slander, {and} abusive speech from your mouth."
—Colossians 3:8

When you slip up, don't forget to forgive yourself (and to ask for forgiveness) for being less than perfect.

"Bear with one another and, if anyone has a complaint against another, forgive each other; just as the Lord has forgiven you, so you also must forgive."
—Colossians 3:13

Don't be afraid of your anger. Anger is a feeling, and, as such, it need not be feared. Neither, however, should it be ignored. What we do with anger is the key.

"A fool's anger is known at once,
But a prudent man conceals
dishonor."

—Proverbs 12:16

Many times our anger is a response to feeling threatened, afraid, or out of control. If you can allow yourself the time to feel angry without feeling guilty about it, you will be more at peace in your situation.

"The Lord is my light and my salvation; whom shall I fear? The Lord is the stronghold of my life; of whom shall I be afraid?"
—Psalms 27:1

Deal with your angry feelings by taking them to prayer and asking for healing. By letting go of them, you can help keep your heart open and receptive to the love and care that is around you.

"So, remove grief and anger from your heart and put away pain from your body, because childhood and the prime of life are fleeting."

—Ecclesiastes 11:10

We cannot—nor would it be a good idea to—eliminate anger entirely from our lives. When we accept the fact that our anger has something to teach us about ourselves and life in general, we neutralize its power and free ourselves to find the wisdom it offers.

"The effect of righteousness will be peace, and the result of righteousness, quietness and trust forever."

—Isaiah 32:17